Contents

Chapter 1 2

Chapter 2 6

Chapter 3 10

Chapter 4 16

Chapter 5 20

Chapter 6 24

Chapter 7 28

Chapter One

Friday night is always chicken and chips night for Mum, Lela and me. Wee Ling makes the best. You should taste them!

"Chicken pieces and portion chips for Mark," calls out Wee Ling.

That's me. I make a dash to the counter, pick them up and tuck them under my arm. Outside, it's getting dark. Usually, walking on my own in the evening doesn't bother me. I've done it heaps of times. But tonight it seems spooky. The mist hangs around, making the lights in the houses look like mean yellow eyes, and it feels like they're all watching me.

I try to stop the creepy feeling overtaking my thoughts, by thinking about other things. It would have been good if Mum had let me buy some ice cream to have for afters, but that's like asking for a holiday on the moon.

Still, at least I didn't have to bring my little sister with me tonight. When I take her, I have to walk really slowly. But without her, all I can hear is the echo of my footsteps. The street is strangely quiet. I clutch the packet of chicken and chips. It feels warm under my arm.

Then suddenly... POW! Out of the blue, or more like out of the mist, I get the strongest feeling that I'm being followed. Don't ask me why. I just do.

I sneak a quick look over my shoulder (not that I can see much).

I start to motor around the corner into Fox Street. Who'd want to follow me? And what for? I've hardly got any top secrets, except the one about Mr Pedosky.

Mr Pedosky lives next door to us. He's real ancient and he's got a glass eye. Mum told me he lost his right eye in the war. She told me not to stare at it, but now that I know, I've noticed that the glass eye doesn't move. Anyway, I reckon, Mr Pedosky is a really mysterious person – scary.

I try to stop my own scary thoughts as I run across the street. The person following me is getting closer. It's not that I'm scared. Well... not really. It's just creepy not knowing who it is. Then a thought hits me. It's probably just someone from the stupid Snoopers Club. They are always

playing tricks on everyone and trying to stir things up.

At that moment – from out of the mist – a dark shape jumps me. "Got you!" it hisses.

Chapter Two

I nearly collapse with fright, until I realize that the dark shape is Scott, my best friend.

"What did you do that for?" I yell. "Now look what you've made me do." The packet of chicken and chips lies on the ground. As I bend down to pick it up, I hear a small sound a few paces behind. Another enemy. Right! Whoever it is can start the count for a showdown.

"Sorry..." starts Scott.

"Shush!" I say, pulling him down beside me.

"What is it?" he whispers. "What did you grab me for?"

"One of the Snoopers," I say, pointing in the direction of the sound. "Been following me. Time for a showdown. You in?"

Scott nods.

"OK, now," I say in a soft voice.

We pounce. The air is full of loud cries as Scott and I land on the enemy. But it's not a Snooper. It's a mangy cat!

I thought you said it was one of the Snoopers," says Scott, in disgust.

"Y'ouch!" I exclaim, trying to disentangle myself from the wild ball of fuzz clinging to me. "Get off..."

The cat is not very big. But its claws are like needles. "Scram!" I hiss, once I'm free.

"Whose cat is it?" asks Scott.

"Don't know," I say, making a fast track back to get our takeaways.

"It's following you."

"What!" I exclaim. "Not again. What's its problem?"

"Maybe it's looking for a home," says Scott.

I shrug. "It's no use. Mum wouldn't want to know. Cats are top of her *Most Unfavourite Animals* list."

Then Scott says a smart thing. "I bet it's after a piece of chicken."

I tuck the packet under my arm. "Well, it's not getting any."

Just then, Scott's mother calls out. She's got a voice like a loudspeaker. "Scott! Scott!"

"Coming," he turns to me. "Gotta go," he says in a whisper.

I grin. Poor Scott. Last time Mrs Rapson came to the school, you could hear her loud voice all over the place.

"See you," he says.

"Don't forget our club meeting tomorrow," I remind him.

Scott nods and waves, then disappears into his house before his mother can start yelling again.

Our club is discussing how we can make a counter-attack on the Snoopers for our sports day next week. Last year, the Snoopers started a fruit-juice rage and guess who got the blame?

Chapter Three

When I finally make it in the back door to the kitchen, Mum is cross.

"What took you so long?"

"Saw Scott," I say.

"You see him a hundred times a day." She shakes her head. "I don't know what you two talk about."

"Sorry, Mum," I mumble, hoping desperately she doesn't notice the dirty marks on the chicken-and-chips packet, where it hit the ground.

Next second, my little sister is squealing and pointing at the scraggy ball of fur that's sneaked into the kitchen behind me.

Hey, Fuzz! Give us a break!

The cat takes no notice of my frantic telepathic thoughts. It is now sneaking up to Mum. It's about to rub itself up against her legs. I can't watch. Don't do it, Fuzz! Get a life!

But it's like it's got a death wish.

For a split second, my mind blanks out, like it's totally not there. Then I dive into action. I rush at the cat. It gets such a fright, it flies up Mum's back. She lets out an ear-splitting screech. The chicken and chips go sky-high. Lela claps her hands and laughs out loud.

In the middle of all this, our neighbour Mr Pedosky appears. Even in normal times I reckon that Mr Pedosky looks like a vampire. He's got long front teeth and he's always shouting stuff about us kids *curdling his blood*.

Standing in the dark doorway, Mr Pedosky looks like he's just stepped out of an old movie. He's got a dark coat on and he is wearing a black patch over his glass eye.

I drop the cat. It disappears behind the rubbish bin. Mum yells.

Mr Pedosky says very calmly, "This is not a good time. No?"

"What? Is something wrong?" asks Mum. Her voice is pins and needles.

"Um. No. Yes. Ah, may be..." Mr Pedosky's voice trails off.

"Mark!" says Mum, interrupting Mr Pedosky's dithering. "Get that cat out! And when you've done that you can start picking up the takeaways."

Anyone would think everything was my fault – like I brought the cat home deliberately.

"I'll come back," says Mr Pedosky.

"No, no. Come in," says Mum, using her quiet voice – the voice that I have now learnt from experience is the voice she uses when she's really fuming inside. (One day, I reckon, she'll go up in flames.)

Mr Pedosky is still hanging around the doorway. That's the big difference between him and a real vampire – a real one would have sucked out half our blood by now.

I move towards the cat, tiptoe, tiptoe, slowly, slowly. Then WHAM! Before it can draw a single claw, its life in our house is over.

The two of us fly past old Pedosky (who's still hovering between night and day) faster than a zap of lightning, faster than a turbo football, faster than my friends leaving the classroom at the end of the day.

When I reach the far end of the yard, I dump the wild animal. Then I shoot back inside, before it can get any more ideas about following me.

Chapter Four

Five minutes later everything is calm. We're at the table eating our chicken and chips. Yuck city. Hard chips and soggy chicken. And cold! Mum cleaned them with a tea-towel before we were allowed to touch any. Mr Pedosky is telling us a sad story about his glass eye. He doesn't seem worried that my ears are flapping, taking in all the gruesome details.

"I am putting my eye on the bench." He takes a mouthful of the strong coffee Mum made him. "I do some other things. Then I am wanting to put it back... but it is gone." He pauses and looks at me fiercely.

"My eye, is not there. It is not anywhere. It has just vanished."

"Well, it can't have vanished," says Mum. "It must be somewhere." She leans over and removes a bit of chip that Lela's busy mashing into her hair.

"I look all over. But it's hard..."

"Yes. Of course," says Mum hurriedly, in case Mr Pedosky decides to give us a full-on description of life with one eye.

"I am thinking..." continues Mr Pedosky, "that it is running away somewhere."

I giggle. Pictures of a glass eye with little legs running away fill my head. Then I quickly change the laugh into a cough, when I see Mum frowning at me. But the pictures won't go away. Maybe Mr Pedosky's eye has gone to visit other glass eyes.

Imagine. They'd all be cross-eyed staring at one another. I splutter and an explosion of chips and giggles comes out before I can stop it.

Mum glares at me. "Mark will be happy to help you look for it."

Oh, yeah! Mark, the great "glass-eye hunter". Why does my mother volunteer me for things that I don't want to do!

"Won't you!" says Mum, smiling.

Mashed spiders. Red rats. Blah soup. "I guess," I mumble.

It's not that I don't like Mr Pedosky or anything. But my favourite TV show is on in five minutes. It's up to a real exciting part. Now I'll probably never find out where the jewels are hidden.

"Mark!" says Mum, interrupting my thoughts. "Off you go."

I open my mouth to ask if later would be OK, but Mum's face tells me she's "brewing a storm". So, off I go with Mr Pedosky into the night.

Chapter Five

We squeeze through the hole in the hedge that Mum uses when she visits Mr Pedosky – she says it takes too long to go right round the street. Mr Pedosky's back door is wide open.

"Ah, strange," he mutters.

I stop. "What! What's strange?" I ask. My voice crackles.

"The door," he says. "I did not leave it open this much."

Oh great! Now there's probably an intruder in on the act as well. "I'll go first and see," I whisper, hoping that Mr Pedosky will stop me – hoping he'll pull me back.

Instead, he says, "That is good."

Knees knocking, I move towards the house, slower than a bike with no wheels. I creep inside the house, my heart thumping. The kitchen is in darkness. I hear a scuffling sound. What is it? I wait. No more sounds. Go, hero! Get the light! I put my hand round the door…

SPIT. SPLAT.

I flick on the light switch. Yep. I knew it. That fuzz doesn't know when to give up. We give each other the fish-eye stare for about half a second, then I lunge. But before I can grab the pest, it goes behind the oven.

Mr Pedosky comes in. "I am hearing..."

"It's OK," I say. "It's the cat..."

Mr Pedosky interrupts. "I am thinking it is hungry. Poor thing." He goes over to the fridge and gets out a carton of milk.

I shrug. Well, if he wants to make a fuss over it, that's fine by me, but I want to get back to my TV show. If I'm not too long, I could still see some of it. "Whereabouts was your eye before it got lost?" I ask.

"Over there," says Mr Pedosky, pointing towards the kitchen bench.

Chapter Six

I search high and low, but there's no sign of the glass eye. I don't like to say it, but I reckon it's rolled down the plughole.

Old Pedosky seems more interested in pouring milk into a saucer and putting it down on the floor, than discussing the situation. "Here, Puss," he says, kneeling on the floor and peering with his one eye into the gloom behind the stove.

"I can't find it," I say.

But Mr Pedosky isn't listening. It's the fuzz all the way. A pink nose, two bright eyes and bunches of whiskers are sticking out from behind the oven.

Talk about looking halfway decent. What a con artist. It's got Mr Pedosky completely fooled.

"A long time ago, I had a cat," says Mr Pedosky.

"Mum hates them," I say.

At the mention of Mum's name, the fuzz disappears behind the oven again. I go back to the matter of the glass eye. "Maybe I can come back tomorrow. Do another search then."

Mr Pedosky nods. "That is all right." I'm halfway to the door, thinking about my TV show when RRRRRRrrrrrrrr. Something rolls out from behind the oven. A black paw follows. SWAT. SWAT. Across the floor, the thing goes – followed by the black and white fuzz. What the...?

SWAT. SWAT.

The thing rolls in my direction, and stops. I look down. Help! Murder! An eye stares back at me.

"Ha!" says Mr Pedosky, smiling, his large front teeth in full view.

Chapter Seven

As I bend to pick up the lost eye, I'm beaten by a paw. Again, Mr Pedosky's glass eye rolls across the floor. Then the cat, halfway to following it, suddenly smells the milk. Game forgotten, it makes a beeline for the saucer. While it's busy guzzling, I crawl under the kitchen table and pick up the small ball of glass. Totally, totally weird.

I bet there're not many people who can say they've held an eye in their hand. I give it to Mr Pedosky. But he hardly notices. He's too busy making a fuss of the fuzz. And the fuzz is making the most of it! Sly-paws!

Later that same night, I'm lying in bed, grinning – I bet in a million years you'll never guess what about. I'll give you a clue. It's something to do with Mr Pedosky and what he gave me for helping him to find his eye. Three guesses what it is. Nope. Not a biscuit. Nor a bit of cake. It's nothing to do with food. Money? Dream on! Mr Pedosky's hardly got enough for himself. And now, with keeping the fuzz, he's going to have even less.

You give in?

OK, here goes. Mr Pedosky gave me his very first glass eye. How's that for brilliant?

FROM ELIZABETH PULFORD

Is there a real Fuzz? Absolutely! Just like Fuzz in the story he was a scraggy kitten that had been dumped. Eleven years later, the Fuzz is still with us. And the man with the glass eye? Well... I was ten years old when I met a man with a glass eye that squeaked when he rubbed it. I nearly fainted when he took it out and I saw this eye looking at me from the palm of his hand...

FROM JOHN BENNETT

Fuzz was modelled on my own cat Silj (pronounced Seal-ee), who shared much of the feisty nature of Fuzz. I think that my fond memories of him surface in these drawings and help to make the book *Fuzz and the Glass Eye* special to me.

Fuzz and the Glass Eye

ISBN 13: 978-0-79-011699-0
ISBN 10: 0-79-011699-5

 Kingscourt

Published by:
McGraw-Hill Education
Shoppenhangers Road, Maidenhead, Berkshire, England, SL6 2QL
Telephone: 44 (0) 1628 502730
Fax: 44 (0) 1628 635895
Website: www.kingscourt.co.uk
Website: www.mcgraw-hill.co.uk

Written by **Elizabeth Pulford**
Illustrated by **John Bennett**
Edited by **Sue Ledington**
Designed by **Kristie Rogers**

English Reprint Edition © 2011 McGraw-Hill Publishing Company
Based on the original edition © 1997 Shortland Publications

All rights reserved. No part of this publication may be reproduced or distributed in any form or by any means, or stored in a database or retrieval system, without prior written consent of the publisher, including, but not limited to, network or other electronic storage or transmission, or broadcast for distance learning.

Printed in China through RRD, Hong Kong.

The McGraw·Hill Companies